Dog Days

by
Annie Hulley

Dog Days was given its world premiere at Theatre503 on
the 28th of February 2014 in a co-production between
Theatre503 and Anchra Productions

Published by Playdead Press 2014

© Annie Hulley 2014

Annie Hulley has asserted her rights under the Copyright, Design and Patents Act, 1988, to be identified as the author of this work.

A CIP catalogue record for this book is available from the British Library.

ISBN 978-1-910067-06-2

Printed by BPUK

Playdead Press
www.playdeadpress.com

Dog Days by Annie Hulley

CAST

John Wilson	Jonathan Oliver
Cate Wilson	Annie Hulley
Tony Bell	Peter Bramhill
Hayley Stevens	Lashana Lynch

CREATIVE TEAM

Director	Lisa Cagnacci
Designer	Sophia Simensky
Lighting Designer	Christopher Nairne
Sound Designer	John Leonard
Composer	Timon Wapenaar
Assistant Director	Dom Riley
Graphic Design	Holly Williams

PRODUCTION TEAM

Producers	Theatre503 and Chris Clough
Assistant Producer	Aine Flanagan
Stage Manager	Simon Batho
Production Manager	Aine Flanagan
Press Representative	James Leaver at Target Live

Annie Hulley | Cate Wilson

Annie Hulley won a scholarship to train at The Bristol Old Vic Theatre School and since then has worked extensively as an actress performing at the Royal Court, The Bush, Bristol Old Vic, The Crucible, The Kings Head, Hampstead, The Bridewell, York, Leeds, Liverpool and Oxford playhouse amongst others. For television she is best known for her role as Karen Moore in Emmerdale and Gwen Loveday in Coronation Street. Her recent television credits include Dates, Sirens, Skins. Annie's many other TV appearances include The Royal, Sweet Medicine, Born and Bred, The Queens Legs, We The Accused, L S Lowry, Casualty, Getting On, Campion, The Bill, Kinvig, The Dig, City Central, Sloggers, September Song, London Bridge, Sleepers, The Specials, Return Of The Antelope, A Pinch Of Snuff, Eldorado, Doctors, A Brother's Tale, Teach Yourself Gibberish, Send in the Girls, Ain't Misbehavin' , Sounding Brass, Spend, Spend, Spend amongst many others. Films include: The Roymann Closure, It Could be You, Ulysses. Annie also works extensively as a voice over artist.

Jonathan Oliver | John Wilson

Jonathan trained at Manchester University. His recent theatre roles include: One million tiny plays about London (Royal Festival Hall) Brecht's

Berlin Kabaret (Soho Playhouse), The Spire (Salisbury), The Merchant of Venice (Creation Theatre Company), Resolutions (Theatre 503), Antony and Cleopatra (The Nuffield Theatre). Jonathan is also a seasoned actor for Factory productions and has worked at Nottingham, The Palace Theatre Watford, The Crucible, Library Theatre Manchester, The National Theatre. Television credits include: Agincourt, Angel of Death, The Gentleman Thief, Eskimo Day, The House of Elliott, King of the Ghetto, Call Me Mister, The Detective, The Bill, Hannay and The Sea Green Man amongst others. Films: Burning Ash, Death Watch, The Return Of The Jedi. Jonathan also works extensively as a voice over artist.

Peter Bramhill | Tony Bell

Peter trained at the Welsh College of Music & Drama. Theatre Credits include: Life for Beginners (Theatre503). The Phoenix of Madrid & The Surprise of Love (Theatre Royal Bath). Geoffrey Bernard is Unwell (Theatre Royal Bath). The Woman in Black, King Lear (Young Vic and Liverpool Playhouse), Much ado about Nothing (Regents Park), An Inspector Calls (Oldham Coliseum), The Glass Cage (Royal & Derngate Northampton),The Miniaturists (The Arcola Theatre), Taming of the Shrew (Wilton's Music Hall) Thomas Moore (The Royal Shakespeare Company) (Ian Charlson Award nomination). For the Royal Shakespeare

Company, Believe what you will, Sejanus, Speaking like Magpies and Othello. Gone Donkeys (The Bush Theatre). Macbeth (For the Ludlow Festival), Bone in the Teeth, (The Bush). Terrence McNally's Corpus Christi in Edinburgh and London. Christopher Wren's highly-acclaimed premiere production of Swithboard. The Grace Theatre. Antony & Cleopatra and As you like it for Michael Bogdanov's English Shakespeare Company. "Stranger in the Night (Salisbury Playhouse) and A Christmas Carol at the Birmingham Rep also directed by Michael Bogdanov. Film credits include Mind Flesh, The Nugget Run, Justin Kerrigan's Human Traffic, Jump for Simon Fellows and Love Roy. Television credits include Doctors, Father Brown, Wickedest, Vexed, Dustin Baby, Made with Magic, Eastenders, Holby City, The Bill and Footballers Wives

Lashana Lynch | Hayley Stevens

Lashana graduated from Arts Educational School of Acting, London, with First Class BA Hons. In her second year she received the Laurence Olivier Bursary Award. Upon graduating she played the leading role, Mende Mazer, in Slave at Lowry Theatre, for which she was nominated for Manchester Evening News Award for Best Newcomer. Lashana then went on to play one of the leads, Belle Newman in British movie Fast Girls. Last year, Lashana played Tybalt in Romeo and Juliet at Royal National Theatre, and Martha in the Olivier Award winning play studios), Burning Bird (Unicorn Theatre), Oranges on the Brain (Pegasus Oxford), You and Me (Greenwhich Theatre) Film includes; Screaming Guns (Director Dave Nolan). At the Finborough Theatre, Sophia was costume designer for Events Whilst Guarding the Bofors Gun, Production designer for An Incident at the Boarder, Operation Crucible and Associate designer for Carthage (2014)

Lighting Designer | Christopher Nairne
Recent theatre credits include: Our Ajax, The Busy Body and Someone Who'll Watch Over Me (Southwark Playhouse), Dracula (for Theatre Royal Bath), The School for Scandal (Park Theatre & Theatre Royal Bury), The Ghost Hunter (Old Red Lion Theatre & UK tour), Recording Hedda (New Diorama Theatre), Fiesta: The Sun Also Rises and Celebrity Night at Café Red (Trafalgar Studios), Boy in a Dress (UK tour) and A Dish of Tea with Dr Johnson (Out of Joint, UK tour & Arts Theatre). He was also Re- lighter for Complicite's 2013 UK tour of Lionboy. Opera work includes: Vivienne (Linbury Studio, Royal Opera House), The Crocodile (Riverside Studios), La Bohème (OperaUpClose; 2011 Olivier Award winner), Albert Herring (Surrey Opera) and The Cunning Little Vixen (Ryedale Festival Opera). Cabaret work includes numerous shows for acts such as Morgan & West, Frisky & Mannish, Shlomo and The Vocal Orchestra.

John Leonard | Sound Design

John started work in theatre sound over 40 years ago and during that time he has provided soundtracks for theatres all over the world, written an acclaimed guide to theatre sound, won various awards and published several collections of sound effects. He is a Fellow of The Guildhall School and an Honorary Fellow of The Hong Kong Academy Of Performing Arts. Recent theatre: Mystae (Hampstead Theatre Studio), Shiver (Watford Playhouse), Moon Tiger (UK. Tour), Rapture, Blister, Burn (Hampstead Theatre), Ghosts (Almeida & West End), The Duck House (Tour & West-End); A Little Hotel On The Side (Theatre Royal, Bath); Quartermaine's Terms (West-End); Other theatre includes: Old Money, Farewell To The Theatre (Hampstead Theatre); Ghosts, Turn Of The Screw, The Dark Earth & The Light Sky, Filumena (Almeida Theatre); Untold Stories, (National Theatre and West-End), Detroit, London Assurance (National Theatre); Birthday, Tribes (Royal Court); Ghosts, A Day In The Death Of Joe Egg (Rose Theatre, Kingston) One For The Road, (Northampton Theatre Royal), Bully Boy (Northampton Theatre Royal & St. James Theatre, London), Ladies In Lavender (National Tour), Heresy Of Love (RSC); amongst many others in the UK and USA.

Timon Wapenaar | Composer

Timon Wapenaar is a South African composer resident in Spain, whose music embraces a wide variety of styles and influences, from traditional South African Boeremusiek to the High Baroque. He has collaborated with top South

African artists, producing arrangements for zef rave sensations Die Antwoord and the Johannesburg Philharmonic Orchestra for their joint performance at the South African Music Awards, as well as for singer Arno Carstens. His most recent work for the theatre includes two Theatre503 productions: "Billy Chickens is a Psycopath Superstar" and "Anansi: an African Tale".

Dom Riley | Assistant Director
Dom graduated from Durham University in 2012 and is Artistic Director of Quirk Productions. Theatre includes: as writer/director, Island State (Edinburgh Fringe/Waterloo East), Misconduct (LOST Theatre/Waterloo East); as co-director, The Copla Musical (Collisions Festival, Central School of Speech and Drama). Writing for theatre includes: The Weatherman (Arcola), Guardian Angel (Little Pieces of Gold, Park Theatre)

Aine Flanagan | Production Manager / Assistant Producer
Aine Flanagan is a freelance producer, production and marketing manager. She has recently produced the critically acclaimed "Margaret Thatcher Queen of Soho" (Theatre503) and the sell out series of "Brain of Brittain" events (Theatre503), previously she toured shows extensively in both Ireland and the UK and worked at Theatre503 as part of their Resident Assistant Producer scheme. As well as working on Dog Days she is also currently developing several other projects to bring to the Edinburgh Fringe Festival and abroad.

Simon Blatho | Stage Manager

Simon trained at The University of West London. Theatre Credits include: Company/Deputy Stage Manager Seussical (Arts Theatre), Stage Manager (John Lloyd: Life of Liff (So Television), Stage Manager Rory McGrath & Philip Pope: Bridge Over Troubled Lager (So Television), Stage Manager Angels in Heels (Tabard Theatre), Company Stage Manager Waiting for Stanley (Finger in the Pie), Technical Operator Mosquito Note (Theatre 503), Stage Manager DayBreak (Notion Theatre), Artist Liason West-End Live (Trafalgar Square), Stage Manager Captain Stirrick (Rose Theatre Kingston), Stage Manager IYAF Raise the Roof (Rose Theatre Kingston), Technical Crew Sleeping Beauty (ATG Richmond Theatre), Deputy Stage Manager Pride London (Trafalgar Square Main Stage 2010/2011), Venue Manager International Youth Arts Festival (Kingston, Studio101). Upcoming projects include the 2014 UK tour of Avenue Q.

Theatre503 is the award-winning home of groundbreaking plays.

Lead by Artistic Director Paul Robinson, Theatre503 is a flagship fringe venue committed to producing new work that is game-changing, relevant, surprising, mischievous, visually thrilling and theatrical. Our theatre is one of London's few destinations for new writing and we offer more opportunities to new writers than any theatre in the country.

Theatre503 Team:

Artistic Director – Paul Robinson
Executive Director – Jeremy Woodhouse
Producer and Head of Marketing (maternity cover) – Polly Ingham
Associate Artistic Director - Lisa Cagnacci
Literary Manager – Steve Harper
Literary Coordinator – Graeme Thompson
Resident Assistant Producers – Natalie Goodwin, Helen Matravers
Senior Readers – Lauretta Barrow, Chris Bridgeman, Catherine Edwards, Jimmy Osborne
Intern –Annie Callahan
Literary Intern – Matt Sandford
FOH Co-ordinator - Vanessa Garcia
Development – Michael Levy, Jill Segal
Associate Directors – James Dacre, Gemma Fairlie, Tom Littler
Associate Artist - Johanna Town

Shine a light on Theatre503...
Theatre503 receives no public subsidy as a venue and we cannot survive without the transformative support of our Friends. For as little as £53 a year you can help us remain *"Arguably the most important theatre in Britain today"* (Guardian).

Becoming a Friend of Theatre503 is simple. Annual support donations are invited in four tiers:

FOOTLIGHT
£53 (less than £5 per month)
Priority notice of productions and events
Special ticket offers
E-mail bulletins
Programme credit

SPOTLIGHT
£253 (or £21 per month)
as Footlight, plus:
Priority booking for all productions
Seasonal updates
Two complimentary tickets to 503 in-house productions
Complimentary invitation to play readings

LIMELIGHT
£503 (or £42 per month)
as Spotlight, plus:
Credit in all published play texts
Complementary invitations to Galas
Programme signed by cast
A credit on a plaque in the foyer.
A complementary play text or signed script
Two complementary tickets to all productions
An invitation to attend rehearsals of a 503 in-house production

HIGHLIGHT

£1003 (or £84 per month)

as Limelight, plus:

Seat reservations

Invitation to the Dress Rehearsal of a 503 in-house production

Annual party for up to ten of your guests at a performance including tickets and refreshments

All donations go towards the running of Theatre503 and enable us to continue to produce important new plays and launch exciting new writers. If you would like to become a Footlight, Spotlight, Limelight or Highlight Friend please visit our website, email **info@theatre503.com** or call us directly on **020 7978 7040**.

Dog Days would not have been possible without the help of so many people

Keith Bartlett, Roland Smith and all at Theatre Delicatessen, Chris Smyrnios and all at Southwark Playhouse, Cat Willis, Ryan Gage, Tony O'Callaghan, Jacqueline King, Jack Clough, Graham Kent, Professor Trevor Walker, David Horovitch, James Leaver and all at Target Live, Paul, Jeremy, Polly, Steve and all at Theatre503.

SETTING

The living room of a small-detached house. The exterior of the house, like the interior, is in a neglectful state. The garden is overgrown and the whole property has a run-down feel to it. In estate agents parlance 'the house is ripe for refurbishment'

TIME

The action takes place over the summer.

DOG DAYS

ACT 1

SCENE 1: HOUSE: AFTERNOON

The lights come up to reveal a sitting room. It is shabby and somber. On the right is a window. Back stage right is a door. An archway, centre left, leads into a small kitchen area with direct access into the rear garden.

JOHN in shorts is sitting at a table (centre) looking through paperwork whilst eating his lunch.

CATE can be heard calling from the kitchen.

CATE: (O.S.) If you want that garden tidied up, you can do it yourself. It's so hot out there next door's chickens are laying hard-boiled eggs.

There is a loud clatter from the kitchen.

CATE: (O.S.) (CONT'D) For god's sake how many more times...

CATE enters from the kitchen brandishing a teaspoon.

CATE: (CONT'D) ...stop putting teaspoons in the sink. It leaves a stain... not good for house selling.

JOHN: *(dismissive)* Viewers, of which we've had several, have never mentioned stains in the sink as a reason for not putting in an offer.

JOHN glances around the room.

JOHN: (CONT'D) *(sarcastic)* I mean why would they... given the splendour of this little palace?

JOHN returns to the spreadsheets.

CATE shakes her head and sighs.

CATE: You wonder don't you... why this home sweet home of ours... is so squalid now... how it got like this... don't you wonder?

JOHN: You used to run this place like a ship. Weren't allowed in with shoes on, had to take your coats off... put them on colour coded hooks I seem to remember... yours was green, mine was blue and Paul's was red.

CATE: You seem to forget, because mine was red… yours was green and Paul's was blue.

CATE takes a sandwich from JOHN'S plate and starts to eat.

JOHN: *(ploughing on)* I'm going through the finances and for ease of reference I've printed this off for you.

JOHN pulls out a piece of paper.

JOHN: (CONT'D) What I've done on this spreadsheet, is to include a proposed income from you. I've put that in a separate column.

CATE peers down at the spreadsheet whilst still eating.

CATE: I don't have an income… you said what I earned was an insult. So I didn't want to keep insulting you.

JOHN: That was then, this is now and things have changed. You've got a degree, even if it is only in Domestic Science it would still help get you something. You could go back to Marks and Spencer's. It may mean working on the shop floor initially but it

would be a start... even cleaning toilets is
a beginning.

*CATE throws the remains of the sandwich onto the table. It
lands on the spreadsheet.*

JOHN is irritated.

JOHN: (CONT'D) What did you do that for? It's
covered in grease now. It's obliterated
some of the figures.

JOHN wipes the spreadsheet and removes the sandwich.

CATE: Well fiddle with some more figures. It's
what you like doing, whilst Rome burns.

*JOHN shakes his head despairingly and goes back to the
spreadsheet.*

JOHN: *(matter of fact)* What I'm proposing is a
clean break. We...

CATE: *(interrupting, knowing)* I thought this was
supposed to be a 'trial separation'
...temporary.

JOHN: *(defensive)* Yes, but... we need to have a
base from which to move forward... to
know where we stand... just in case.

CATE: *(pointedly)* Just in case what? Things don't work out?

JOHN: *(sharp)* It's prudent to be prepared for all eventualities. *(beat)* What I'm proposing is a clean break. A 50/50 split. Obviously there'll be pieces of furniture that can't be divided, so what I'm suggesting is that we draw lots.

CATE: You mean like at an auction?

JOHN: Like a raffle. We itemise everything, write it down, and then take turns to draw tickets.

CATE: What if I win things in the raffle /auction... that I don't want?

JOHN: Then you can either a) offer them to the other party or b) get rid of them.

CATE: Would I have to pay to get rid of them?

JOHN: It would be your responsibility yes, as equally it would be mine.

CATE: Then I refuse to cooperate.

JOHN frustrated gathers his paperwork together.

JOHN: It's pointless trying to reason with you when you're in this mood... determined to be belligerent.

CATE: I'm not determined to be anything... I'm merely stating that I would rather choose the items that I want after twenty-eight years of collecting them... rather than draw them out of a raffle!

JOHN exits towards the kitchen.

JOHN: When you've come up with a better solution... let me know. In the meantime, I'll be in the garden, trying to beat a path to the greenhouse. It's so overgrown; Tarzan could swing out there.

CATE: I could swing out there. That would give the neighbours something to talk about... grief stricken woman caught swinging from the branches in suburbia, eating bananas and hobnobbing with orangutans. Why not, let's live a little?

JOHN: No one's interested in your life anymore... don't you kid yourself.

JOHN exits out through the kitchen.

CATE slumps on the sofa. The doorbell rings. She ignores it.

CATE takes out a cigarette. The doorbell rings again.

CATE: Damn...

CATE strolls to the door, holding the cigarette.

TONY, suited and booted and HAYLEY all height and eyeliner, are on the doorstep. They are an attractive couple even if there is something 'in your face' about them.

TONY: I hope you don't mind us dropping by... only we were just passing and saw the for sale sign. We wondered if we could have a look round if that's convenient?

CATE: It's not convenient.

HAYLEY: We won't intrude.

TONY: It'll only take a few minutes. Mrs. er?

TONY and HAYLEY step over the threshold.

CATE reluctantly lets them in.

CATE: Wilson. Cate Wilson.

HAYLEY: What a beautiful room!

HAYLEY gazes around her.

HAYLEY: (CONT'D) I love the curtains... could we come to some arrangement about the curtains if we were to...

TONY: *(interrupting)* Steady on, don't jump the gun. We've only just stepped over the threshold. There's a lot to see yet isn't there Mrs. Wilson?

HAYLEY leans against the table and starts to fan herself.

HAYLEY: Can I have a glass of water? I feel a bit giddy.

CATE: I'll get you one... but then you'll have to leave I'm afraid. We don't do unaccompanied viewings.

CATE exits into the kitchen.

HAYLEY: It's hotter than two rats shagging in a sock in here.

HAYLEY sits on the sofa.

CATE can be heard calling out.

CATE: (O.S.) John… some people are here.

JOHN: (O.S.) What?

CATE: (O.S.) *(irritated)* Viewing people!

HAYLEY: I love it though Tony… even if it is shabby. I feel we were drawn here by some subconscious force.

TONY: Don't go overboard baby doll.

HAYLEY: *(determined)* I want this house. I could do so much with it. Look at the state of the place!

TONY: Baby whatever you want… you shall get.

HAYLEY: That's why I love you Tony. You always do the best for me. We're a team… it's us against the world.

HAYLEY embraces TONY full on.

CATE re-enters with a glass of water.

CATE: *(embarrassed)* …erm…

HAYLEY and TONY break off.

CATE hands the water to HAYLEY.

CATE: (CONT'D) I've put some ice in it.

TONY: She needs cooling down... not that I'm objecting to having a hot chick on my arm... am I babes?

TONY pats HAYLEY'S bottom playfully.

HAYLEY: *(teasing)* Don't be sexist Tone.

TONY: Sexist... you love it!

TONY laughs. He turns to CATE and is businesslike.

TONY: (CONT'D) We couldn't help notice the shabby frontage... it hasn't exactly got... what is it they say on those property shows babes?

HAYLEY: Kerb appeal.

TONY: That's right... it hasn't got that.

HAYLEY: We both want to put our own stamp on things anyway. You know, clean lines an' that. Mixing contemporary with traditional, sleek décor... vibrant colours...

TONY: *(interrupting)* Yeah, yeah babes we get the picture *(to CATE confidentially)* She watches a lot of those property shows.

HAYLEY: Kirsty and Phil... I feel like they're my mates.

TONY: Well they're not.

HAYLEY: I got a signed book.

TONY: What's that got to do with anything?

HAYLEY: It makes it more personal don't it?

TONY: It makes them fucking richer! *(beat)* Excuse my French Cate... I forgot myself... lady like you... I need my knuckles rapped. If my old man were alive he'd smack me round the head with a baseball bat.

HAYLEY looks at CATE appraisingly.

HAYLEY: *(disingenuous)* You look really good for your age. How old are you fifties, sixties? You look great either way. It must be your genes.

CATE: I'm not meaning to be rude… but I think you should come back another time… with the estate agent.

CATE tries to usher TONY and HAYLEY out.

TONY: I don't like estate agents…not top drawer. I wouldn't trust 'em with me Hamster.

HAYLEY: Have you lived here long?

CATE: A lifetime.

HAYLEY: Thing is… we've seen over twenty houses and this fits the bill lovely. You've got off street parking as well. That's a great feature… very Victorian.

TONY: What beats me is why move when you've got a place like this? *(with humour)* What is it Cate, cracks in the marriage, cracks in the plaster… children left home… which one?

CATE: All three.

TONY: *(amused)* You're a joker… I like that.

JOHN enters from the garden. TONY approaches him.

TONY: (CONT'D) We were just passing… saw the for sale sign. I'm Tony Bell and the other half's Hayley… pleased to meet you… er…

TONY offers his hand.

JOHN: John Wilson.

JOHN shakes TONY'S hand. There's something awkward about it.

TONY: Like the shorts John… very Bermuda.

JOHN: *(slightly thrown)* Thank you… erm… what do you think of the house, going to buy it?

TONY'S mobile rings.

TONY: Apologies.

TONY answers his mobile. He makes no attempt at discretion.

TONY: (CONT'D) …yeah mate… not now ok… I'll call you… yeah… I know there's a lot of money at stake… and no-ones more keen to nail that motherfucker than me…

HAYLEY crosses to the kitchen arch and looks through. She talks over TONY's ad lib phone conversation.

HAYLEY: Ooh... granite worktops... brilliant for hot pans. All your knick-knacks, aren't they sweet? Those little owls... my Nan used to collect owls. My granddad binned them all one day. It broke her heart. He said he couldn't stand the sight of them anymore and couldn't stand the sight of her anymore... and cleared off.

CATE and HAYLEY move off into the kitchen.

TONY ends the call. He shakes his head.

TONY: Sorry about that John. There's a board meeting tonight and they can't sneeze without me.

JOHN: What are you on the board of if I may ask?

TONY: I would tell you John but it's top secret. *(TONY laughs)* Only joking.

There is an uncomfortable pause.

JOHN: Can I er... get you anything?

TONY: A whisky please John.

JOHN is slightly taken aback.

HAYLEY: (O.S.) You've got a lot of shelves. I love shelves… cos then you don't have to keep opening cupboards.

JOHN pours a small whisky.

TONY: So how much you want for the house. I'm not talking asking price, I'm talking bottom line price.

JOHN: You'd have to discuss that with the estate agent.

JOHN begrudgingly hands TONY the Whisky.

TONY: Let's do a deal… avoid commission. Tell the estate agent you've changed your mind about selling… we buy it… cash gets exchanged and bingo… everyone's a winner.

JOHN: We're too far down the line for that. We've got further viewings later this week.

TONY: Had quite a few have we… and no takers? How long's it been on the market then?

33

JOHN: A couple of weeks, early days.

TONY: That's odd because it was first listed three months ago… and it's got a reduced price on the Internet. I looked before I came.

JOHN: I thought you said you were just passing.

TONY: *(thinking on his feet)* You've got to check things out though, haven't you John?

JOHN: I see… well… we went in high initially… to test the waters.

TONY: *(straight in)* I could put cash in your hand by the end of the week… no messing. Hayl's and I, are unencumbered buyers… we can move at the drop of a hat *(confidentially)* Word in your ear John… don't get caught in a chain… link after link until some dick brain falters and the whole fucking shooting match comes tumbling down. If I were you, I'd bite my hand off right now.

JOHN: Well… erm… I'm sure we could possibly come to some arrangement if the price was right.

TONY hardly listening moves to the door.

TONY: I wouldn't mind a look upstairs… before I make you an offer you can't refuse.

JOHN: Oh sorry I thought Cate would have shown you.

TONY: Not my place to entice your wife up to the bedroom is it John?

TONY laughs as he exits with JOHN.

HAYLEY and CATE enter talking.

CATE: *(bored)* The utility room is only three years old. We added it on to make the kitchen bigger. You couldn't swing a cat before.

HAYLEY: *(new idea)* We might change it into a garden room. Put in a hot tub. I've always wanted one of those, you know for when friends come round. Everyone having a little dip, letting loose… eating Ben and Jerry's. They're great for chillin'. Celebrities have them. Do you read 'Hello' magazine?

CATE: I've browsed through it once or twice, when I've been to the hairdressers.

HAYLEY: I read it every week. It's where I get my ideas from, about lifestyle issues and stuff.

JOHN and TONY enter from the hall.

TONY: *(animated)* John and I have been talking business upstairs. He's going to take the house off the market. We're buying it!

JOHN: Subject to contract of course.

TONY: Subject to a horses head being found in your bed… and no one wants that, do they John?

HAYLEY: Oh Tony I love you so much… I knew this was the one… I knew it!

HAYLEY rushes over and embraces TONY with passion.

CATE and JOHN look on, ill at ease.

END OF SCENE

SCENE 2: HOUSE: (NEXT DAY)

HAYLEY is looking around the room, enthusiastically taking photographs with her phone. She has a notebook and a tape measure with her. She is calling out to CATE in the kitchen.

HAYLEY: I can't wait to move in. Tony say's I'm like a whirlwind when I get excited. Even the teachers at school used to call me 'the tornado.' Mind you I didn't get excited there very often. *(proudly)* I was a low achiever.

HAYLEY continues snapping as CATE enters with two coffees.

CATE: Not everybody's academically orientated. I wasn't... although I was very good at making 'cauliflower au gratin'.

CATE hands HAYLEY the cup.

HAYLEY: Thanks for letting me come round today.

CATE: You certainly don't let the grass grow... it was only yesterday you put in your offer.

HAYLEY: I've already been looking at furniture. I saw this gorgeous red sofa this morning... that's why I need to do a quick measure...

HAYLEY gets out her tape measure.

HAYLEY: (CONT'D) ...would you mind holding the other end?

CATE takes the other end of the tape measure.

HAYLEY starts taking measurements and writes them down.

HAYLEY: (CONT'D) I think it's going to fit... it'll be big... but Tony and I like snuggling up on the sofa. Do you and John still snuggle up?

CATE: No, we've never been the snuggling up type... we're more Alaskan in our displays of affection.

HAYLEY: Well you know what they say; if you don't use it... you lose it.

CATE: I'll remember that. Thanks for the advice.

HAYLEY: I get a lot of yeast infections...that's the downside. I put garlic up there. It's a natural remedy... gives you garlic breath though... cos it travels up. I don't tell Tony. He just thinks I've been eating a lot of Jerk chicken.

CATE: I've never tried that.

HAYLEY: What garlic up your fanny?

CATE: Jerk chicken.

HAYLEY: They're both good.

HAYLEY stands back admiringly.

HAYLEY: (CONT'D) That sofa's going to look lovely in here. Just as well, cos it costs a fortune... but Tony says I can have what I want.

CATE: All husbands say that but what they mean is, within the rigid parameters of their wallets.

HAYLEY: Partner. We're not married. Tony doesn't believe in marriage on account of his parents. They were low life scumbags, used to lock him in a cupboard.

CATE looks concerned.

CATE:	What kind of cupboard?
HAYLEY:	An ordinary cupboard... you know for household appliances an' that. He'd be in there for hours. He reckons that's where his personality was formed... you know his darker side... still it's good for business... him being a bit ruthless.
CATE:	What does he do, your partner?
HAYLEY:	He runs an escort club... arranges 'things' for visitors. If someone wants a nice restaurant, Tony will book it, He'll arrange cars, hotel rooms, Poker games. That's how I met him; I was a receptionist at the Portland. I work at the club now... nothing sexual... not even blowjobs. *(beat)* I'm not that keen on work now to be honest... not with the baby coming.
CATE:	Oh, you're having a baby? That's wonderful.
HAYLEY:	I'm so happy. Tony was a bit odd about it at first... but he loves the idea now. It was his idea we look for a place together. A home... for a family.

CATE: This is a perfect house for bringing up children. There's a good school and the parks just round the corner. I used to take Paul there... (*she trails off*)

HAYLEY: Paul... is that your son?

CATE: (*quietly*) Yes.

HAYLEY: Is that him... in the photograph over there?

HAYLEY crosses over to the photograph and picks it up.

HAYLEY: (CONT'D) He's very good looking. Mind you I've always had a soft spot for men in uniform... especially soldiers. They're so manly aren't they?

CATE: (*distant*) Yes... they are.

HAYLEY sits next to CATE who is thoughtful.

HAYLEY: What was giving birth like? (*beat*) Rita, the woman who does my Brazilians, said it was like shitting a watermelon?

CATE: (*amused*) I don't think that was how the NCT described it. (*CATE smiles*) I remember we had to sing a nursery rhyme.

41

I chose Oranges and Lemons. And Faure's Requiem… as my relaxing music.

HAYLEY: Did it work?

CATE: I ended up screaming like a banshee and swearing like a trooper.

HAYLEY: I reckon I'd be like that only worse. I'm definitely going to have an Epidural.

HAYLEY rubs her pregnant stomach and sits down.

HAYLEY: (CONT'D) My baby's a boy… me and Tone were determined not to find out the sex… 'let nature reveal itself' we said… but as soon as the nurse said 'do you want to know?' We both said 'yes' straight off. *(beat)* I've got a photograph of the scan in my bag…

HAYLEY gets the photograph out and shows it to CATE.

HAYLEY: (CONT'D) You can just make out his tiny little widget…

HAYLEY points at the photograph. CATE peers closely.

HAYLEY: (CONT'D) Tony said 'well he don't take after me in that department'.

HAYLEY laughs and puts the photograph away carefully.

HAYLEY: (CONT'D) Tony's got a mono brow... I hope the baby don't take after him in that department either.

CATE looks at her watch.

CATE: I'm going to have to hurry you I'm afraid, I... er... need to start the dinner.

HAYLEY: Can I join you? I'm starving. Tony can pick me up from here. He's working late tonight. I hate being on my own... especially with the baby coming.

CATE: Well, erm...

HAYLEY: I could do your nails if you like. I'm good at manicures.

END OF SCENE:

SCENE 3: HOUSE: (LATER ON)

Remains of food are on the table.

HAYLEY is filing CATE'S nails.

JOHN is reading, clearly agitated. He looks at his watch.

JOHN: It's gone ten... what time was Tony picking you up?

HAYLEY: It depends on whether he's gambling or not. You know what it's like, winning streak, losing streak?

JOHN: Fortunately I don't. I'm not a gambling man.

HAYLEY continues CATE'S manicure. They both ignore JOHN.

HAYLEY: I'll bring my nail kit next time... do you a Union Jack or something... or a Daisy... I can do those.

The doorbell rings.

JOHN jumps up.

JOHN: At last.

JOHN lets TONY in. TONY is slightly drunk.

TONY: Mon amies... I bring great news! Mr. 'high rollin fucking pavlova', that Russian geezer... has been taken to the cleaners... by cool hand Tony here.

TONY gestures with his fist.

TONY: (CONT'D) Back of the net!

TONY kisses HAYLEY. She is not impressed.

HAYLEY: I hate it when you gamble Tone. I hope you're not going to do that when we've had the baby.

TONY: I'll be a reformed character by then babes. I guarantee it.

JOHN: *(straight in)* We've all got early starts in the morning... I'm sure.

TONY: Do you fly fish John?

JOHN: *(scoffing)* Fly fish? No I don't. It's a bit urban round here for fly-fishing.

TONY: Shame, it always looks so exciting on those nature programs, grappling with the rapids, grappling with the fish... never letting go of your catch John, never letting go.

JOHN: Yes, well I'm sure it's all very interesting and I wish you all the best with it... sorry to have to rush you out.

TONY: Not at all. Don't want to out stay our welcome... even if it is our house.

JOHN: Not yet.

TONY: Only joking John. Having a bit of fun, nothing to worry about.

TONY takes CATE'S hand and kisses it.

TONY: (CONT'D) A pleasure as always Cate.

TONY and HAYLEY exit. JOHN is disgruntled.

JOHN: *(sarcastic)* Thanks for that... Hayley's bloody company... like a bad night in a youth club!

CATE: *(looking at her nails)* She's very good at manicures... she's given me square edges... whatever that means.

JOHN: What is it about you women and a bit of pampering... you fall for it every time? Manicures, pedicures, creams... it's all a waste of money. Why can't you just accept you grow old like everybody else?

CATE: Because we don't want to end up looking old and ugly like you. Mr. super jowl!

JOHN: That's one thing I can be grateful for... that you've let yourself go... much easier on the purse strings.

CATE: I'm off to bed. I want to try to get to sleep before the onslaught of your snoring. I shan't miss that when I've got my own place... your bedtime version of 'Hello Dolly'. It's a showstopper!

CATE goes to draw the curtains. She stops and peers out.

CATE: (CONT'D) Their car's still there.

JOHN: Whose car?

CATE: Tony and Hayley's... it's in the drive.

JOHN: Don't say they've broken down... please God.

47

CATE: No, I don't think that's the problem.

JOHN moves across to the window.

CATE: (CONT'D) I think they're... erm...

JOHN: I can see... legs!

CATE: Akimbo by the looks of things.

JOHN: I'm going out there. I'm putting a bloody stop to this. Pornography in the front drive!

CATE: You can't go out and interrupt them, it's embarrassing. Let's go to bed, pretend we haven't seen anything. They're only young after all.

JOHN: Are you mad... they're shagging in our drive... it's like me going out and urinating in the bushes?

CATE: How do you work that one out?

JOHN: They've got a bed at home. I've got a toilet here... yes? Bloody hell, do I have to explain everything!

CATE: Some people like doing it in strange places. A couple got caught having sex in a car wash last week.

JOHN: Good to know your keeping abreast of the news.

CATE: Well I knew it would come as a surprise to you... other people's amorous adventures... given your sexual bypass.

JOHN: *(fuming)* It's no good. I've had it with them. The deals off... it's the straw that broke the camel's back.

JOHN starts to pour himself a stiff drink.

JOHN: (CONT'D) I'm giving them their fucking marching orders.

CATE: *(taken aback)* Well... if you're sure?

JOHN: Never been bloody surer of anything in my life...

CATE: I don't mind waiting for another buyer.

JOHN: ...one step too far...

CATE: I'm not even sure this 'temporary separation' is a good thing.

There is a pause. JOHN has finally heard CATE.

JOHN: *(backtracking)* What I mean is... the deal is still on... I'm not saying that it's... er... off... exactly...

CATE: But you just said it was off...

JOHN: Not in a real sense... no.

CATE: In what sense then?

JOHN: In... the... sense that it would be bloody stupid not to carry on with the sale... for the sake of them... not understanding what is and what isn't acceptable. *(beat)* It's not as if anyone else wants to buy this dump is it? *(beat)* We're stuck... with babes and Mr. Flash Harry, holding our exit visas. I don't like it. I don't like it one bit... but I don't have any bloody choice!

JOHN exits upstairs in a huff.

END OF SCENE

SCENE 4: HOUSE: (TWO WEEKS LATER)

JOHN is sitting on the sofa, reading. A bottle of wine is on the table. CATE enters from the kitchen carrying a cake with candles (not lit). JOHN looks up concerned.

CATE: *(singing)* Happy birthday to you, happy birthday to you, happy birthday dear Paul, happy birthday to you...

CATE holds the cake aloft.

CATE: (CONT'D) I've put 24 candles on it! Shall I light them?

JOHN: No, of course not. It's insane.

CATE: We're pretending. You agreed.

JOHN: I wasn't being serious.

CATE proudly puts down the cake and starts to cut it.

CATE: How big a slice do you want?

JOHN: I don't want any.

CATE: Should I cut three pieces anyway?

JOHN: If it would make you happy... then cut three pieces?

CATE takes out some party hats.

CATE: I've bought party hats too. Shall we put them on?

JOHN: Absolutely not.

CATE: *(undeterred)* Then I shall wear two.

CATE puts on two paper hats. JOHN watches her concerned.

JOHN: Cate... pretending like this... it's not healthy. I...

CATE: *(interrupting)* You're not eating your cake and it's Paul's birthday.

JOHN: I don't want to eat it. I've been very clear about it.

CATE ignores JOHN and continues to eat her cake.

CATE: I'm going to make my fish pie for tonight. Paul used to love it. Said it was the coconut milk that made all the difference.

JOHN: I don't remember that. You're imagining it.

CATE: I thought I'd make it as a treat, for his birthday.

JOHN: But he's not here to eat it. Like he's not here to eat this cake.

Cate, with a flourish, puts her cigarette out in the centre of the cake.

JOHN: (CONT'D) What did you do that for?

CATE takes off the party hats and scrunches them up.

JOHN: (CONT'D) *(sighing)* Living like this... it's not doing either of us any good. The sooner we get this sale done and dusted the better.

JOHN picks up the cake and takes it into the kitchen.

CATE pours herself a large drink.

CATE: *(sarcastic)* But you're hardly ever here these days. You're always in Birmingham having meetings... about paper clips.

JOHN re-enters.

JOHN: There's talk of redundancies and I don't want to be in the firing line. I've got enough on my plate selling this place.

CATE: You seem very keen, very driven to push this sale through. Are you that desperate to get away from me?

The doorbell rings.

JOHN goes to answer the door.

JOHN: Let's just er... leave this for now... we don't want to... air our dirty washing in public.

CATE: What dirty washing?

TONY and HAYLEY enter.

HAYLEY is holding a potted plant.

JOHN is surprised to see them.

CATE continues with the conversation. She is insistent.

CATE: (CONT'D) What dirty washing? I don't know what you mean.

TONY: Not interrupting anything are we? Lovers tiff and all that. We can always come back another time… if you want to kiss and make up… use the bedroom facilities…?

JOHN: *(embarrassed)* No no no no. It's nothing like that. We were… just… er…

CATE: …airing some dirty washing… but I don't know what dirty washing we were airing…

JOHN: *(clenched teeth)* It's just a figure of speech… no need for close examination.

CATE: But…

JOHN: *(snarling)* Leave it. *(beat)* What can we do for you?

HAYLEY offers the plant to CATE.

HAYLEY: I won this at a raffle for prostate cancer. My mate Linda works at the hospital. Thing is I don't have anywhere to put it. It's a shrub apparently and when it flowers it looks like little white hankies.

CATE: That's very kind of you.

HAYLEY: It's not a present... ooh... I feel embarrassed now. It's just that I wanted to plant it in your garden, which will be my garden... eventually. Would you mind?

CATE: Of course not. Follow me. It's a bit of a jungle I'm afraid...

HAYLEY and CATE move off towards the garden.

TONY sprawls on the sofa, puts his feet on the coffee table.

JOHN looks affronted.

JOHN: Excuse me... but would you mind taking your feet off the table?

TONY: Sorry John... forgot where I was for a minute... must be because I feel at home already.

TONY notices the bookshelf.

TONY: (CONT'D) You a big reader John?

JOHN: A bit of a book worm... yes.

TONY: Too much joined up writing for me... I prefer action rather than words.

JOHN: Pity your preference for action doesn't translate itself into the house buying process.

TONY: That's down to the professionals John... white-collar men... not dissimilar to yourself. Once those pen pushers get involved... it's a slow boat to China. Thing is...

TONY sits upright.

TONY: (CONT'D) *(suddenly serious)* ...there's a problem with the survey. Several of the roof supports have dry rot.

JOHN: *(amused)* Dry rot... sure that's not what you're talking?

TONY: Very funny John, very droll... but you know what they say... don't give up the day job. *(beat)* You know who you remind me of... my math's teacher at school... we used to call him Rudolph because of his red nose, bulbous, a drinkers nose... he was like a human calculator. There was nothing he couldn't add up... and we're not talking two and two. That's who you remind me of John, old Rudolph... on his beam end now old Rudolph... demon drink brought him to his knees... you never know how life's going to pan out do you?

JOHN: I'm not a math's teacher.

TONY: Pity, maybe you missed your vocation in life... either that or joining the military. You command respect and that's no mean feat in this day and age I'm telling you.

TONY nods his head in respect then comes in hard.

TONY: (CONT'D) Thing is, there has to be a reduction in the price.

JOHN: There was a reduction, as you well know. It was on the Internet, prior to your initial viewing.

TONY: Yes but that was a general price reduction and not a specific one Johnnie boy... fair do's!

JOHN: *(goaded)* You know something? I'm not even sure you're serious buyers? *(beat)* Just because you flatter my wife doesn't mean you can take me for a patsy... understood?

TONY: Understood John, well and truly. If there were a bible, I'd swear on it.

TONY stands to attention, saluting, mocking.

TONY: (CONT'D) Yes sir, I salute you!

JOHN: And tonight when you leave, which I hope will be sooner rather than later... I'd prefer it if you didn't copulate in my drive.

TONY: Ah...

JOHN: It's not that we were prying...

TONY: I see...

JOHN: We were drawing the curtains in our own home.

TONY: You're making me feel bad now John, ashamed almost. There was I thinking me and Hayl's were having a private moment when all the time you and your wife were watching.

JOHN: We weren't watching, we were drawing the curtains like I said. What you and the blushing mother to be were doing... was an arrestable offence.

TONY: Indecency, in a public space?

JOHN: Exactly.

TONY: That's why we were in your driveway... to avoid any such exposure. It's not as if we were on the public highway is it? That would have been a different story... passers-by and that.

JOHN: Is that your way of apologising, for your obscene behaviour?

TONY: I don't feel my behaviour was obscene... making love to my beautiful babes. When passion takes you... it takes you... don't you find?

HAYLEY and CATE enter through the kitchen.

HAYLEY: *(to John)* You've got a family of foxes living down there. Shit everywhere, enough to bath in.

HAYLEY and CATE move into the room. HAYLEY crosses to TONY.

HAYLEY: (CONT'D) *(excited)* We could move the patio from the top... build a new one at the bottom... put in electricity and a barbecue. You know, one of those integrated ones... so it just sits in the garden wall...

TONY: *(interrupting)* But you've got a nice kitchen, all integrated. You can barbecue in there, on the grill, like in the old days.

HAYLEY: It's all about alfresco dining now in it?

TONY: Yeah, right, freeze your bollocks off dining.

HAYLEY: We can get one of those patio heaters, that'd soon warm it up.

TONY: What's the point in heating a kitchen outside, when you've got a perfectly warm one inside? That babes... is daft!

HAYLEY sits on the sofa in a huff and sulks.

TONY: (CONT'D) Women! Never happy unless they're raiding your wallet are they John?

TONY turns to CATE flirtatiously.

TONY: (CONT'D) Present company excepted of course.

TONY lights two cigarettes. He offers one to Cate.

CATE hesitates and takes it.

TONY: (CONT'D) The thing is, sometimes I feel like I'm invincible. If someone comes up to me and gives me grief, I feel this like, 'white heat thing'…and then anything could happen. *(beat)* Any ashtrays Cate?

CATE: I've hidden them, in an effort to stop.

TONY: It doesn't appear to be working.

CATE: No, it's clearly failing.

CATE reaches an ashtray from above the bookshelf. As she does so a bottle of Vodka runs into view.

CATE, seen by all, takes a deep swig from the bottle.

TONY watches.

JOHN is displeased.

JOHN: That's helpful. You swigging neat Vodka at six in the evening.

CATE: A momentary lapse…

CATE takes another swig.

CATE: (CONT'D) I apologise if I offend but I can't get it out of my head... this 'dirty washing' business.

JOHN: *(short)* Not now Cate.

CATE: I suspect it's something to do with our 'trial separation', which it has to be said, has all the hallmarks...of a cleaver, slicing through a piece of meat... never to be rejoined.

TONY replenishes CATE'S glass.

TONY: It's us who need to apologise, for our cavorting in your drive last week. I think the French would call it... a crime of passion.

CATE: Unusual for this neck of the woods... passion. *(beat)* I live alongside a passion bypass... did you know... was it in the property particulars?

JOHN: My wife, as is obvious to all but the most stupid... is clearly intoxicated... worse for wear...

JOHN starts to usher TONY and HAYLEY out.

JOHN: (CONT'D)...so thank you for calling round ...glad we've been able to talk things through... my solicitor will be in touch with yours first thing...

CATE: What's the hotel like?

JOHN: What?

CATE: In Birmingham?

JOHN: What the bloody hell's that got to do with anything?

CATE: I'm only asking... no need to bite my head off.

JOHN: *(sharp)* Hot rooms, bad pillows, intermittent Internet, the usual. Happy now?

JOHN ushers TONY and HAYLEY to the door, urgently.

CATE: Do you spend much time there? I've often meant to ask about your other life... but it keeps slipping me by. Do you... spend much time in your room?

JOHN: I have a curry in a hurry and then crash out. What is all this, twenty bloody questions?

CATE: I'm just curious that's all. Why are you being so aggressive?

TONY: 'Me thinketh the man doth protest too much'.

JOHN: What's that supposed to mean?

TONY: It's a famous Shakespeare quote John.

JOHN: *(with sarcasm)* Is it really, thank you for sharing that with me? *(beat)* Now, if you would kindly be on your way... as you can see my wife is totally deranged...

TONY: *(stirring it)* What's the name of the hotel you stay in John? I know 'Brummie' quite well... might be able to negotiate you a discount... I do a lot of business with hotels.

JOHN: The Grange, I doubt you'd know it. It's a boutique hotel.

TONY: Ah... grandiose.

JOHN: Exclusive.

HAYLEY: I thought you said it was basic... with bad pillows and intermittent Internet?

JOHN: *(covering)* What I meant was... it's not five star... but it's comfortable.

TONY: Old fashioned... plush interior?

JOHN: Yes.

TONY: Central to all amenities?

JOHN: Very handy for the centre, yes.

TONY: *(in for the kill)* Closed down last year. I knew the owner... cashed in his chips. Lives in Barbados now with a trophy wife... massive tits...

HAYLEY: Implants probably... know how you tell? Implants stay upright when you lie down whereas real boobs get squidged under your armpits.

TONY: Babes, you know I love talking about boobs... but in this instance... I'm more interested, in learning about John's predicament.

CATE: I'm interested in learning about John's predicament too... very much so.

JOHN: I don't have a predicament. It's just that I can't always remember things.

CATE: You can't remember the name of the hotel you've been staying in for the last 18 months?

JOHN: Not exactly no, sometimes I've stayed at other places.

TONY: You're getting in deeper John.

JOHN: Shut your mouth.

TONY: Word to the wise... when you're in a hole... stop digging.

JOHN: Fuck off!

There is a moment.

CATE: You know what I think... I think you've been having a bit on the side... with some tart... who doesn't mind two second sex and bad breath.

HAYLEY: I know lots of girls who don't mind that. They'd say that was a result.

CATE: Prostitutes.

JOHN: Don't be ridiculous.

HAYLEY: Have you tried Viagra... keeps you erect for hours. This old bloke I know took some... and he could still hang his jacket on it ten hours later.

JOHN: I certainly don't need Viagra. Nor do I need to discuss my sex life with you! I have no problems in that department thank you very much!

CATE: Yes you do... I've been married to you for twenty-eight years and I know.

JOHN: *(goaded)* Well that's with you my dear.

There is a silence.

JOHN: (CONT'D) With Lucy however, I'm a bucking bronco...

TONY: *(enjoying it)* Mind your backs! Shit is about to fly.

CATE: Lucy?

JOHN: *(resigned)* I've been... having... a relationship. We met at work. *(hesitant)* We're in love. There it is... I've said it now. You've pushed me to say it.

TONY: You should never admit to anything John... first rule of being accused.

JOHN: Will you please... stay out of my affairs!

CATE: *(shocked)* A relationship?

JOHN: *(hesitant)* Yes. Look Cate, I'm... sorry. I...

CATE: *(shaken)* But... you said, when we first talked about this 'trial separation' ...that there wasn't anyone else...

JOHN: I didn't want to hurt you... I was worried... your state of mind...

CATE: I asked you specifically, if there was anyone... and you said 'no', it was a 'space thing'...

JOHN: Well it is… in a sense… space for me to get away from you and for you to get away from me.

CATE: Let me get this right… whilst I was thinking, you were having life and death meetings in Birmingham about staplers and things… you've had your trousers round your ankles… shagging the office slut!

JOHN: This isn't the time or the place.

CATE takes a moment.

CATE: Does she wear short skirts?

JOHN: *(weary)* What? *(beat)* Not particularly. She wears trousers a lot of the time and cashmere.

CATE: Cashmere. Does she wear it next to the skin?

HAYLEY: Very itchy next to the skin Cashmere… like Angora… although I'd never wear that 'cos of the little rabbits.

JOHN: I think she wears a singlet thing underneath. What does it matter?

CATE: A singlet?

HAYLEY: There's a campaign on to ban the fluffy fibre.

JOHN: You know a vest type thing.

CATE: Like the ones I've got in different colours?

HAYLEY: I've signed a petition.

JOHN: I didn't know you had any singlet tops.

CATE: *(saddened)* But you know she wears cashmere.

JOHN: Yes... I suppose... I dunno...

CATE: What kind of shoes does she wear... heels?

JOHN: Yes heels. What is all this?

CATE: Does she kick them off as soon as she's home?

JOHN: She has a footbath. It keeps her feet soft. I've tried it... it's very relaxing

CATE: You, a footbath?

JOHN: *(almost indignant)* Yes.

CATE grabs the bottle of Vodka.

CATE: Well I'd never have guessed... you... Mr. Tootsie toes...

CATE leaves abruptly.

HAYLEY: There's a bloke I know called Cornelius... he's got the biggest toes I've ever seen... has to wear individual socks over them...

There is a moment as they ponder this. TONY regroups.

TONY: Sounds like she's a classy bird, John... this Lucy. I'm not averse to a bit of foot massage myself. Reflexology, just another reason for jerking off in my book.

HAYLEY: I'd better see if Cate's all right. It's probably the menopause. My Aunty Vera's went on for twenty years. She was so hot once; she ended up in the freezer cabinet at Tesco's. She just got in with the fisherman's pies. They weren't very pleased the Tesco people... food contamination they said. I think they were overreacting... cos she took her shoes off.

HAYLEY follows CATE out. TONY watches HAYLEY leave.

TONY: They're all mad... women. I get a double whammy with Hayley cos she gets hysterical as well. Her sister's the same, runs in the family.

JOHN: Unfortunate.

TONY: You got any John? *(beat)* Family?

JOHN: A sister, younger in Durham.

TONY: Cold up there is it?

JOHN: I wouldn't know.

TONY: Not close?

JOHN: Not particularly.

TONY: Chalk and cheese?

JOHN: I wouldn't go as far as to say that.

TONY: When was the last time you saw your sister? Did she come to your wedding?

JOHN: It was a long time ago. I can't remember who was there.

TONY: Didn't she approve of the bride?

JOHN: It wasn't a question of that.

TONY: I wouldn't worry about your infidelity John... it's clear that Cate's no wallflower. Take it from one who knows... I can recognise a woman on heat in an instant. Mind you, she's a tidy piece your wife. I bet she raised an eyebrow or two... in her youth... little mini-skirts and all that. Still it's difficult for a woman of a certain age. She looks like she needs re-assurance, that she's still attractive. Sure she's not getting that re-assurance somewhere else? I mean is she really a woman of virtue? So few of them are. Most of 'em are dirty little alley cats. I bet you know what I mean... man like you, of your standing... having a bit on the side it's only right and proper.

TONY puts his arm around JOHN and speaks intimately.

TONY: (CONT'D) ...I'd like to invite you to my club one night John, where my girls work. Real class, cocktails, mood music. It's like a different world.

TONY gives JOHN a manly hug and a pat on the back.

JOHN visibly bristles.

TONY: (CONT'D) Like I said before... drop your price and it's plain sailing from here on in.

CATE enters in a sexy dress (too short). She poses.

HAYLEY follows.

JOHN looks horrified.

CATE: This is my Mary Quant dress... my Mary Quant fake dress I mean. The point being that I can still wear it without looking stupid.

JOHN: *(diplomatic)* I'm not sure it still suits you though. I mean it was an entirely different era... and of course we were all much younger...

CATE: *(insistent)* The point being... I can still wear it 30 years later *(Cate sidles up to John)* whereas you can't wear the same trousers you wore thirty days ago... cos you've got a beer belly. I on the other hand am as flat as an iron around the stomach area... aren't I Tony?

CATE demonstrates her flat stomach.

TONY: As flat as a pancake. No question.

TONY lights two cigarettes and hands one to CATE.

HAYLEY: Yeah... that's what I said when I first saw you... that your genes were good. They are, aren't they John... good genes?

JOHN: *(losing it slightly)* Everyone's got good bloody genes except me... isn't that right Cate?

CATE: *(deadpan)* You've got shit genes.

There is a pause.

TONY: Have you eaten Mrs. W? Shall I get us a takeaway? Nice Chinese eh? What d'you say? It's the least I can do... bit of champers to wash it down... push the boat out. It's a night to celebrate after all. A new home, a baby on the way, new friends. I've got some Bruce Springsteen in the car... it's what your generation likes isn't it... a bit of Bruce? We could play that. Have a bit of a dance?

TONY takes CATE'S arm. He twirls her round and round.

CATE starts to laugh loudly.

END OF SCENE:

SCENE 5: HOUSE: (LATER)

Remains of takeaway. Music playing in the background. Bottles of booze are on the table.

TONY and CATE are dancing.

HAYLEY is next to JOHN.

All except HAYLEY are drunk.

HAYLEY: *(shouting)* People have told me that when the baby gets big I'll have bladder problems... on account of it pressing.

The track finishes.

CATE and TONY sit down, exhilarated.

HAYLEY: (CONT'D) I don't want stretch marks though. I want to look good when I'm older. That's why I work out a lot. I've got sixteen tracksuits, four leotards and twelve pairs of leggings, all in different colours.

TONY stands in the centre of the room and announces.

TONY: We'd like you to be Godparents!

There is a silence.

JOHN: To the baby?

TONY: Of course to the fucking baby John, what else? Cheers.

TONY raises his glass and drinks whilst pouring CATE a drink.

JOHN: Well we're very flattered but...

TONY: That's settled then. We can't think of anyone better can we Hayley?

HAYLEY: No, there's only my sister and she's not right in the head. It's really sad but you can't choose your family can you?

JOHN: I'm sorry but we can't be Godparents. We simply don't know you well enough and when we've sold the house, our liaison will have ended, apart from forwarding the odd letter. We'll redirect the mail of course... but the odd one will get through no doubt.

CATE: *(enthusiastic and loud)* I'd love to be a godparent!

JOHN: Don't be absurd. You hardly know them. *(to Tony)* No offence intended.

79

TONY: No offence taken.

CATE: I'll do what I please from now on with or without your permission! You have no influence on my life anymore. You are 'persona, fucking non grata' and don't you forget that!

JOHN: You're drunk! A woman of your age... you're a joke Cate, a sad pathetic joke.

CATE is displeased. She turns and approaches JOHN.

CATE: This Lucy... what in god's name does she see in you... this coffee guzzling nymphet... when she straddles you over the Nespresso machine? That's her isn't it? Coffee queen... lots of froth... shagging you after.

JOHN: I don't know what these mad rants of yours mean... obviously on some subterranean level... way below the gutter... you have an agenda.

CATE: The woman at work who likes coffee! She was called Lucy. Wasn't it her who suggested you get a Nespresso machine? Was that the woman... ol coffee swilling juicy Lucy?

JOHN: *(defensive)* Yes it was her actually. God you've got a vicious way, of going about things… saying things…

CATE: I have… when you've been having it off at every lamppost like a dog… for the last eighteen months!

CATE crosses over to JOHN making dog lapping/panting noises.

HAYLEY suddenly retches loudly.

HAYLEY: I'm feeling a bit queasy. I shouldn't have had those prawns. I think I'm going to be sick.

HAYLEY dashes off.

TONY goes with her, calling after.

TONY: Hayl's, Hayl's… babes… you all right?

CATE watches as they leave and then turns again on JOHN.

CATE: How old is she, your squeeze… your little lap dog?

JOHN: *(resigned)* Well this may surprise you but we actually celebrated her fiftieth birthday last week.

CATE: What would surprise me about that?

JOHN: Because nine times out of ten a man leaves his wife for a younger model.

CATE: But not you? What a star!

CATE sits. Lights a cigarette.

CATE: (CONT'D) So, what did you do for her fiftieth, you said 'we celebrated it'?

JOHN: *(uneasy)* Nothing much.

CATE: I'm interested. What did you do?

JOHN: *(hesitant)* I took her to... Paris.

CATE: *(surprised/shocked)* Paris! Ah...

CATE feigns thinking. She shakes her head.

CATE: (CONT'D) I don't think we went to Paris for my fiftieth. If I remember correctly, Paul and I went out for a Pizza in the end, because you were stuck at the office with some minor crisis or other. What was it again... oh yeah... the printer had a paper jam or something... something like that anyway... you know, something crucial.

JOHN: You've always been very scathing about my work.

CATE: Not just about your work.

JOHN: I'm really perplexed as to what you ever saw in me...

CATE: It perplexes me too...

JOHN turns to CATE.

JOHN: Look, I never meant for any of this to happen...

CATE: *(challenging)* What did you mean to happen then? *(beat)* You hear people say that in Films, TV show... real life now... for me. So, what does it mean exactly?

JOHN: *(irritated)* What do you mean... what does it mean?

CATE: When you were shagging 'ol coffee swillin juicy Lucy' ...what was it... that you didn't mean to happen?

JOHN moves off frustrated. CATE presses.

CATE: (CONT'D) When you were encouraging Paul to join up... what was it... you didn't mean to happen? *(beat)* Is it the same principle, in that you personally instigate things... that you don't mean to happen?

JOHN: Things happen whether I instigate them or not... it's called life Cate... something you opted out of three years ago.

CATE: *(bitterly)* It's not what I would have chosen for myself... that opt out.

JOHN: It's not what any of us would have chosen.

CATE: Yes it is... because you encouraged Paul... you were positively gung ho!

JOHN: Not this again... I refuse to fucking listen to it.

CATE: Paul joined up because of you... that's the truth.

JOHN: He joined up because he wanted to... it was his choice... when are you going to get that, into your demented brain?

JOHN sits down and tries to calm himself.

CATE continues to press hard.

CATE: You wanted him to be a hero. You were happy for him to take the risk, you were proud. *(beat)* It just backfired big time didn't it, your plan to live your sad pathetic paper clip existence through your son?

JOHN: You're unhinged. It wasn't about me! God! How many more times?

CATE: You know what really concerns me... is that you get comfort from believing all this waste was worth it. All the pain... part of the deal... part of what you sign up for and it really pisses me off... that you can think that.

JOHN: You don't know anything about what I think... because you've never asked! Too busy wallowing in the poor me's. *(beat)* But I've got news for you, I wasn't the reason he joined up... it was you who he

85

was trying to get away from... with your constant nagging... your complaining. How did it go again? 'He was so untidy' '...he was so loud' '...he sprawled' ...you used to tell him off for sprawling... he was six foot two for gods sake... you used to tell him off for breathing. It was you who drove him away!

CATE: That's a lie! Asking him to tidy his room wasn't the reason he signed his life away. It was your salesmanship that swung the deal... 'he'd get to see the world', 'be a team player,' 'how it would make a man of him'. You glorified it... sold it well... after listening to you, even I wanted to join up! So don't try and lay your guilt trip on me, because if it wasn't for you, Paul would still be here... and none of this would be happening. You're the one responsible for all this carnage... and that burden; that guilt should weigh you down for the rest of your life!

JOHN suddenly flies at CATE.

CATE hits back wildly. They struggle and crash into the furniture. Bottles and plates fall onto the floor.

JOHN gets CATE around the neck and tries to strangle her.

86

TONY enters and observes the scene. He is casual, like he's seen it all a thousand times before.

TONY: There are rivers of vomit all over your bedroom carpet! I think I'm going to need a bucket.

JOHN, clearly shaken abruptly leaves.

END OF SCENE:

SCENE 6: HOUSE: (THE MORNING AFTER)

CATE is clearing away last night's bottles/takeaway etc.

TONY enters dressed only in his boxer shorts and startles CATE. She drops a plate.

TONY bends down to pick it up. They are face to face.

TONY: Sorry, I didn't mean to startle you.

CATE: You, er, did take me by surprise. *(beat)* How's Hayley?

TONY: Still feeling sick. I wondered if I could have a glass of water, dry piece of toast perhaps, to settle her down.

CATE: Of course.

TONY: Let me help you with all this first.

TONY starts to help CATE clear away last night's detritus.

CATE: I can't believe how many bottles we got through.

TONY: A good time had by all.

CATE: I'm sorry if I embarrassed myself.

TONY: It was good to see you let your hair down.

CATE: I haven't danced in a long time.

TONY: You should do it more often.

They continue to clear. CATE stops. She is clearly embarrassed.

CATE: *(hesitant)* John... er... wasn't really trying to strangle me you know.

TONY: Of course not. It just looked that way.

TONY smiles.

CATE: All married couples have little interludes where... you know... things get a bit... care worn.

TONY: Careworn? Mmmm... that's an interesting word for it.

TONY empties the ashtray.

TONY: (CONT'D) John... is he out a lot... at night?

CATE: Sometimes he has to work late but he's generally back by seven. He's in management.

TONY: Ah... top dog. I thought as much. He'll get a good pension then... mind you he'll need it, for the alimony payments.

CATE: I'd prefer it if you didn't comment on my marriage.

TONY looks CATE up and down.

TONY: Sometimes I forget that I'm in the presence of a lady of culture like yourself. I'm so used to being with ladies with no culture. Lovely girls, don't get me wrong, but... well... I'm institutionalised... what can I tell you?

TONY moves closer to CATE.

TONY: (CONT'D) How fast do you want this to move? You set the pace and I'll fall in. We can go slow or get straight to it. I don't want to rush you.

TONY touches her arm. There is tension.

TONY: (CONT'D) I know what a wrench it must be for you to leave this lovely home. You're a beautiful woman Mrs. W. John is lucky to have you.

CATE: And Hayley is lucky to have you.

TONY: I've been a very naughty boy in the past. On the straight and narrow now though. I'll be honest with you Mrs. W my slate is not completely clean, got caught up in a bit of a tussle, nothing serious, a bit of ABH... but that's all behind me now. *(beat)* Testosterone... too much of it. Runs in the family. I had all brothers you see. They were always slapping me about.

CATE: Were you the youngest?

TONY: Yeah, the little runt. My older brother Tommy... was a sadistic bastard... didn't care what he hit you with.

TONY points to a scar on his forehead. CATE looks.

TONY: (CONT'D) See that? Where he smashed me in the face with a toilet seat. He was a plumber you see... there was always stuff like that hanging around.

CATE: Didn't your mother try and stop him... brutalising you like that?

TONY: My old lady wasn't like you... all homely... she was a right old slag. Always on street corners... with strangers... pitiful.

TONY turns to CATE.

TONY: (CONT'D) You could mother me if you wanted to... in the interim... as a fill in... until your son gets back.

CATE: *(softly)* My son and you are very different... very different all together.

TONY: *(pointed)* I bet we're not that different really, when push comes to shove. *(beat)* You're a deep woman Cate and I can see life's not been kind to you but you never know where destiny may lead. It's all about reciprocal trust and that's why I've invited you into my inner circle... because I trust you with my life... and you can trust me with your life. You're family now Cate, and that's all that matters.

CATE: That's very nice of you Tony... I... I'm... well I'm delighted to be included... be the little ones godmother... I really mean that. You and Hayley are very kind.

CATE turns away and gathers her coat and handbag.

CATE: (CONT'D) I'm going to do some house hunting today. I'll need to lock up before I go.

TONY: We can do that, post the keys through the letterbox when we leave.

CATE: I'd prefer to do the alarm myself, we were burgled once and the insurance company insists the alarm is on.

TONY: Thing is, I'm going to call our doctor just to be on the safe side. I don't want any mishaps... you know... with the baby.

CATE puts on her coat.

CATE: Yes of course. Help yourself to the toast... and there's tea...

TONY: I'll need the code. For the burglar alarm.

CATE: Oh yes... I'll write it down for you.

CATE grabs a pen and writes the code on some paper.

TONY: Oh and the keys... I'll be wanting those.

CATE hands over the keys.

CATE: Make sure you double lock.

CATE exits.

TONY tosses the keys in the air clearly pleased.

END OF SCENE

SCENE 9: HOUSE: (EARLY EVENING)

Music is playing. TONY takes pictures off the walls. He puts CATE'S lamps in a box. He places a throw over the sofa. He puts down a rug.

HAYLEY enters with paintbrush and paint tin, dressed only in a man's shirt. She is wiping her brow.

HAYLEY: Phew... it's hot up there. I've got the first coat on though... duck egg blue... it looks gorgeous. I'm going to have a go at making Kirsty's Lino cut blind next. I've got her step-by-step guide.

TONY: You're obsessed with Kirsty.

HAYLEY: We've got a lot in common.

TONY: What you and Kirsty Allsopp? Don't be daft.

TONY picks up a brightly coloured beanbag.

TONY: (CONT'D) Where do you want this?

HAYLEY: Near the fire... where that disgusting old chair is.

TONY moves the chair and puts the beanbag down.

HAYLEY: (CONT'D) It's looking so much nicer already isn't it... with a few personal touches? *(beat)* Talking of which... where's my infinity picture?

TONY: I'll be honest babes... I don't like that picture... never have. It doesn't look like infinity to me... it looks like nothing.

HAYLEY roots around and finds the picture.

HAYLEY: Well what's infinity supposed to look like?

TONY: I want a picture to tell me a story babe... that's all.

HAYLEY: *(looking at the picture)* My mate Linda who works at the hospital... says they hang this picture in hospices... cos it's uplifting.

TONY: Uplifting if you're dying... fucking depressing if you're not.

HAYLEY: Well we're not having that tennis player girl up... scratching her bum.

TONY: That babes is kitsch.

HAYLEY: What does kitsch mean?

TONY: Anything that's cheap and popular, with a nice arse.

HAYLEY: I knew it... you just like looking at her bottom.

TONY: It's not as good as yours.

TONY kisses HAYLEY'S neck.

HAYLEY: Get off Tone... I want to practise my pushing.

TONY: And I want to practise my shoving.

HAYLEY: I'm serious.

TONY: So am I.

HAYLEY: We've got to do these exercises for breathing... on all fours... for when I have to push...

TONY: Yeah well... I'm not into all that. I like the mystery of giving birth, the magic of it... but not the mechanics... turns me right off babes.

HAYLEY: It's not about you though is it? It's about what's best for the little one. And there's no magic, or mystery... the baby's in there... with a big head and it's got to come out. So just get on the floor behind me... you know doggy style... only don't try anything. It's all about giving birth now.

TONY: It's birds stuff all this babes. I'm not comfortable with it.

HAYLEY: Just do it for me will you? Please Tone... it's only pretending.

TONY reluctantly positions himself behind HAYLEY as she gets on all fours and starts her breathing exercises.

During this exercise regime, CATE enters.

HAYLEY: (CONT'D) ...I've got my legs open... the baby's crowning...

HAYLEY suddenly notices CATE, she jumps and screams.

CATE jumps and screams.

HAYLEY: (CONT'D) Oh my god... you scared me to death... sneaking up like that.

CATE: You scared me to death. What on earth's going on?

HAYLEY: I was pretending to give birth.

CATE looks around horrified.

CATE: Where are all our things?

TONY: We're cheering the place up a bit, adding some 'je ne sais quoi'.

HAYLEY: That's French for taking the eye off the shabbiness.

CATE: Well here's some more French… I like my fucking shabbiness… and you have no right to touch anything… we haven't even exchanged contracts yet! *(beat)* Where are my lamps?

TONY: All boxed up… safe as houses.

CATE: How dare you do this… take such liberties!

HAYLEY: I thought you'd like it. Most people are impressed with my interior design skills. Wait 'till you see the box room… I've painted the walls in duck egg blue… in anticipation of the little ones arrival.

CATE: You'd better not have... they're not your walls to paint.

TONY: You're very touchy Cate... not like you... not like you at all.

CATE: Of course I'm bloody touchy... you're taking over my house.

HAYLEY: *(upset)* I thought it would make you happy... cos I know how rotten John's been to you. I was going to do up the spare room too... for when you come to stay.

HAYLEY grabs Hello magazine from the coffee table.

HAYLEY: (CONT'D) There's a picture in here, of what I was going to do it like... it's Dolly Parton's bedroom... so ignore all the country and western stuff... just imagine all the pinks.

CATE: You're missing the point. You have no right to touch anything.

HAYLEY: You said make yourself at home.

CATE: I didn't mean it literally.

TONY: If you're not happy we can change it all back... nothing's irreversible.

HAYLEY: It would be a shame though, to cover up the duck egg blue. It's taken me all day to paint it.

CATE sighs and sits on the sofa amidst the cushions.

HAYLEY sits next to her and shows CATE the colour chart.

HAYLEY: (CONT'D) What do you think of the colour? I was going to stencil over it... half-moons an' that... make it 'space agey'... for the little one.

CATE takes a moment.

CATE: Is it... Farrow and Ball?

HAYLEY: Dulux satin sheen. *(beat)* Do you want to come upstairs and have a look... it still needs another coat...

HAYLEY and CATE move off upstairs.

HAYLEY: (O.S.) (CONT'D) ...I'm going to make a lino cut blind... you know accessorise it...

TONY helps himself to some of JOHN'S Whisky. He sits on the sofa and puts his feet on the coffee table, totally at home.

JOHN enters talking on the phone. He is shocked.

JOHN: *(into phone)* I'm going to have to call you back... it looks like we've had intruders.

JOHN puts his mobile down.

JOHN: (CONT'D) What the hell...?

TONY: Whisky, John? Nothing like it after a hard day at the office.

JOHN: *(incredulous)* There's obviously some mistake... I thought this was my home.

TONY: A long way to go yet, but it's a start.

JOHN: *(getting angry)* This may come as a surprise to a numbskull like you, but it's normal practice to buy the house first, before starting to decorate.

JOHN starts to throw the cushions off the sofa.

TONY: Now, now John.

JOHN: I want you out!!!!

TONY, calmly, as if in front of a wild animal, puts the cushions back on the sofa.

TONY: Steady on John... no need to get heated.

JOHN: Leave those fucking cushions where they are!

TONY, mockingly steps back from the cushions.

TONY: They're not to everyone's taste I'll admit... but don't you think you're overreacting?

JOHN: Overreacting... are you out of your mind? You barge your way into our home... unwanted, uninvited... you tamper with our things and then have the temerity to suggest that I'm overreacting.

JOHN grabs the throw off the sofa.

TONY grabs the other end of the throw. There is a tug of war. It finally rips in half.

TONY: Hayley won't be pleased.

JOHN: Like I give a damn. Get your things and leave.

JOHN notices the Infinity picture.

JOHN: (CONT'D) What the hell's that?

TONY: Hayley's pride and joy... don't ask. I'm with you, I know nothing about art.

JOHN: That's not art... that's unadulterated rubbish.

TONY: Hayley would be upset if she heard you say that.

JOHN: Take that garbage of my wall... now!

TONY and JOHN don't move. It's a stand off.

Finally JOHN darts across to the wall and takes down the picture.

TONY chases and blocks.

CATE and HAYLEY enter with colour charts, happily chatting.

JOHN darts back across the room with the picture.

TONY tries to bring him down at the legs but misses.

JOHN hurls the picture out of the door.

JOHN: (CONT'D) If you want it... you know where it is. Now, get out the pair of you!

There is a moment.

HAYLEY starts to shake and convulse and make weird noises.

CATE: What's happening?

TONY: She's having an hysterical fit... I warned you John.

HAYLEY appears to get worse.

CATE fetches water and tries to calm her down.

JOHN pushes TONY in short sharp shoves, towards the door.

JOHN: I don't believe any of it... you're just a pair of tricksters nothing more. Chancers... preying on decent people.

TONY stands his ground and starts to wave the keys. JOHN tries to grab them.

TONY fences him off.

HAYLEY watches, after making an instant recovery.

JOHN: (CONT'D) Where the hell did you get those keys you slime ball?

TONY: Mrs. W gave them to me on the strict understanding that I double locked and put the alarm on.

JOHN: She wouldn't be that gullible... not even her.

CATE: I did give him the keys... Hayley was ill... what else was I supposed to do?

JOHN sticks his face into TONY'S.

JOHN: You really think you're clever don't you... Mr slick... soft-soaping a woman too stupid to know better. But as for taking me for a ride... you're way off beam.

CATE: I'm too stupid am I?

JOHN: *(to Cate)* You brought this on yourself... you encouraged it.

CATE: It was you who accepted their offer remember? In a hurry... to set up a love nest... with juicy Lucy.

JOHN: Stop calling her that... it's infantile... and right now...

JOHN starts again, to push Tony forcefully towards the door.

JOHN: (CONT'D) ...it's time for Mr. and Mrs. slime ball to exit out of the gift shop! You've got ten seconds, starting now... then I'm phoning the police. 1... 2... 3...

JOHN continues counting under.

TONY: Johnnie boy, you're really beginning to irritate me you know?

HAYLEY: You're putting us out on the streets, with me expecting?

JOHN: 10! I insist you leave right now!

JOHN gives TONY one final shove.

TONY suddenly angry picks up a fork off the table.

TONY stabs JOHN'S hand with the fork.

JOHN yelps in pain and hops around the room.

JOHN: (CONT'D) You stabbed me!

TONY: Like I said Johnnie boy, you're getting on my nerves.

JOHN: *(in pain)* I don't believe this.

TONY: It was just a fork. Could have been worse. Could have been a knife.

JOHN: You've drawn blood!

TONY: Just a warning that's all. I'll be honest with you Johnnie boy, I don't like being pushed around. My parents used to push me around. Always insisting I did this, always insisting I did that. Makes me very jittery all that insistence stuff. It's not respectful and I have done nothing but show you and Mrs. W the utmost respect. I'm a genuine victim of circumstance and you expect me to turn ourselves out onto the street, with a pregnant woman when you have plenty of room. Does that sound fair to you?

CATE: No that does not sound fair.

JOHN sucks at his hand, clearly in pain.

TONY: Come on John. Let's get you to A&E. I reckon you'll need a couple of stitches...

nothing major... but best to get it looked at. I've got the car outside... but I'd appreciate no blood on the pale leather interior.

HAYLEY: I said you should have gone for the 'ox blood' option.

TONY: I should have listened to you then shouldn't I babes?

JOHN spots his mobile. He goes to grab it. TONY stops him.

JOHN: I'm going to call the police; you've committed assault and any attempt from you in preventing me from doing so...

TONY: *(interrupting)* ...yeah yeah John... we get the message. I'll take you round to the 'old bill' myself... I'll even hand myself in.

TONY puts his hands up in mock arrest pose.

TONY: (CONT'D) It's a fair cop guv... and all that...

JOHN: Your levity is misplaced.

TONY crosses over to JOHN and looks closely at his face.

TONY: You're looking very pale John... we should get you to that hospital.

CATE: Do you want me to come with you?

JOHN: No I bloody well don't. Stay here and help Hayley pack. I want them both out! And I won't take no for an answer.

TONY and JOHN exit.

There is a pause. HAYLEY looks thoughtful. CATE sits, dejected

HAYLEY: I've been thinking...

CATE looks up.

HAYLEY: (CONT'D) ...about cup-cakes. My mate Tracey's, best friend's cousin, Angie... has a cup cake shop in Newport Pagnell. She opened it two years ago... she does wedding cake type cup-cakes as well... she charges a fortune for those. And you know what? She can't cook... not even make toast... at least I can do that... and soup. *(beat)* I want to open a cup cake business... run it from home initially... so I can be with the little one. I've already thought of a trade name... Sponge Gold...

you know like spun gold? I reckon we could make a fortune.

CATE: (*puzzled*) We?

HAYLEY: I'd like you to be my business partner. You could do the baking and I could do the decorating... I'm good at decoration. I really think we'd work well together, compliment each other... and we can take it in turns to look after the little one... you are his godmother after all... it makes sense... don't you think... like it was meant to be?

END OF SCENE

SCENE 8: HOUSE: (THE MORNING AFTER)

TONY is sitting on the sofa with his feet on the coffee table. He is still and quiet.

HAYLEY enters from outside. She sees TONY.

HAYLEY: Oh there you are... I didn't hear you come in last night. What time did you get back from the hospital?

TONY: Late. Where's Cate?

HAYLEY: Strange them keeping John in overnight... did they say anything else to you?

TONY: Only what I told you both on the phone. That it's just a precaution. You can't fart in a hospital these days without it being documented. *(beat)* Where's Cate?

HAYLEY: She went to look at a flat.

TONY: *(urgent)* She's not at the hospital then?

HAYLEY: No, she didn't want to go. She tried ringing John's mobile, 'cos she wants him to sign a cheque or something, but he wasn't picking up... hardly surprising with a stabbed hand.

TONY: It was a graze.

HAYLEY: It did have three fork marks in it Tony! Or was it four fork marks. I've forgotten now. How many prongs in a fork... I've gone blank... can you remember?

TONY: Does it fucking matter?

There is a moment.

TONY: (CONT'D) Where've you been anyway?

HAYLEY: I was talking with the neighbour. She told me something really sad about John and Cate... that Paul, their son died, over three years ago now. He was blown up by an IED in Afghanistan... she showed me this paper clipping.

HAYLEY reads from the paper clipping.

HAYLEY: (CONT'D) 'Two soldiers from the 2nd Battalion The Rifles... were ambushed whilst on a mission to prevent the Taliban targeting their operating base in Nad-e-Ali, Helmand Province. Corporal Stephen Hobson was injured and later had both legs amputated above the knee... and Lance Corporal Paul Wilson died instantly after stepping on an IED... and then it goes on to say other things... that relatives were informed etc.

HAYLEY puts the paper clipping down.

HAYLEY: (CONT'D) There was nothing left of him apparently... just body parts and fragments. They had to take DNA samples to identify him. He was only 21.

Tony takes the paper cutting and starts to read it.

HAYLEY crosses to look at the photograph.

HAYLEY: (CONT'D) When we talked about the photograph... Cate never let on. I wonder why she never said anything?

TONY: It's not the kind of thing you talk about is it... over coffee... a dead son?

HAYLEY shakes her head in disbelief.

HAYLEY: You hear about it happening on the telly... but you never think about it happening in real life to anyone you know... not that I did know him... but I know Cate. *(beat)* He was a war hero, got a medal and everything.

114

TONY: *(with sarcasm)* I'm sure that makes things a whole lot better for the grieving relatives. More respectable.

HAYLEY: No wonder their marriage is in trouble. I don't know how you ever get back to normal living again, after something like that. *(beat)* Do you think I should say anything to her... offer condolences? I don't want to open old wounds. *(beat)* Oooh that's an unfortunate phrase in it? I didn't mean it like that.

TONY: I wouldn't say anything... for fear of unfortunate phrases.

HAYLEY: *(rubbing her stomach)* I don't want the little one joining no army.

TONY: There won't be armies then. It'll all be done by the touch of a button... 'asta la vista baby... lights out!

HAYLEY: Don't talk like that Tone... it's different now we're having a baby of our own. I feel like we've got a responsibility to the world. *(beat)* I'm definitely going to start recycling.

TONY: We'll all sleep much easier in our beds knowing that.

TONY puts the paper clipping out of sight.

HAYLEY: You didn't finish telling me what happened at the hospital anyway.

TONY: They wanted to do 'obs'.

HAYLEY: 'Obs'? You mean obstetrics... I've heard of them.

TONY: *(sharp)* Observations... it's you women who have obstetrics... even I know that.

HAYLEY: I get muddled up with words that's all.

TONY: You get muddled up full stop. Sometimes you seem on a completely different page babes to the rest of the world... like you never take anything seriously.

HAYLEY: I'm serious about the cup-cake business.

TONY: See... that's what I mean. One minute we're talking about atrocities and then next minute you're talking about banalities... in the blink of an eye... like nothing goes deep.

HAYLEY: Things do go deep... that's why I'm thinking of the future... turning a shilling and all that. I reckon I could be very successful at the cup-cake business... lots of women do stuff like that.

TONY: Yeah but they're generally women who can cook.

HAYLEY: You don't need to be able to cook. You just buy a mixture and decorate it and I'm good at decoration.

CATE enters. She has her phone in her hand.

CATE: I keep trying John's mobile but I can't get through. I need to speak to him. *(beat)* I've got some good news for him... I've found a flat to rent... I can be out of his hair. I could move in next week if we get everything sorted... but I need the 'holding deposit' now.

TONY moves away looking for cigarettes.

HAYLEY: He probably can't have his phone on in the hospital. It's their busiest time the mornings... it's when most people die.

TONY: Shifting sands... nothing stays the same...

117

HAYLEY: In any case I've been thinking. You don't have to move out, you could always stay here with us. Couldn't she Tony? We're going to need an extra pair of hands with the baby and the new business venture.

TONY: That's the great thing about being free in life, we can make choices. We don't have to be tied by rules; by convention... we can do and be what the fuck we want to be. *(beat)* Sweet as a nut I say.

There is a pause.

CATE looks preoccupied.

CATE: It was only a graze... mind you John's always been a bit of a baby when it come to things like that...

HAYLEY: It did sever a vein.

TONY: Went in deeper than we thought. Don't know my own strength... do I babes?

HAYLEY: He can bend tablespoons in half.

TONY: Just by looking at them. *(he laughs)* Mind over matter.

CATE: It's unusual though, for a hospital to keep you in, especially over something minor.

HAYLEY: They kick you out as soon as you've had a baby these days. *(beat)* I hope I don't have forceps... I don't fancy being kicked out straight after that... all those prodding things... up your oojamaflip... ughhh...

TONY: *(interrupting)* Enough!! For fucks sake babes... I don't want to know.

HAYLEY: It's different when it comes to the other though isn't it... you want to know then?

TONY lights a cigarette. He is clearly tense.

CATE looks at her phone again.

CATE: I'll call the hospital... John and I've got things we need to discuss.

TONY: Not wise.

TONY takes CATE'S phone.

CATE: What do you mean?

TONY:	Everyone shoots the messenger don't they Cate? Everyone takes a pop at those who bring bad news. I didn't want to tell you last night on the phone... you were upset enough... but he was making his own arrangements... with his visitor.

CATE: His visitor?

TONY: A woman came... Lucy? You know the one... 'juicy Lucy' and it was obvious... that I was no longer wanted. That's why I left and got myself something to eat... so they could be alone for a bit. I didn't want to play gooseberry.

CATE looks shocked.

CATE: Lucy was there... at the hospital?

TONY: *(matter of fact)* He isn't coming back Cate. John's never coming back. He asked me... to deal with things.

CATE: *(unbelieving)* But... he didn't trust you.

TONY: We talked it all through 'look after Cate' he said and Lucy agreed with him... that you would need a lot of looking after. It was clear that they were far from happy about hurting you... but from an outsiders point of view... they were like dogs on heat... you know that lamp post analogy you came up with... very appropriate... very apposite.

CATE slumps onto the sofa. HAYLEY sits next to her.

TONY: (CONT'D) There are some emotions we can't control and lust is one of them. Not that I'm saying their relationship is based on lust alone... because it's clearly deeper than that... but... we're all animals aren't we Cate... you... me... even the Queen? We all play by basic rules, only some are born with a different set of basic rules... I mean like John was born with a different set of basic rules to me and it would be fair and honourable to say that the likes of John despise the likes of me... you know the forward sort, as oppose to the English sort... stand back don't push... that sort. Only me I'm a pusher and a shover and when I'm cornered I don't cower... I fucking fight to the ferocious end. So if I was in the army... inclined to violence like your son was... legitimately so I may add... I'd have been well suited cos then it's ok and acceptable even... to blow the enemy's fucking brains out... like they're a bunch of animals... not people at all. Now there's the rub... how do you differentiate?

CATE: My son's a hero... not a thug... that's how you differentiate!

TONY: Was a hero... but he's dead now and that's a tragedy.

CATE is shaken. HAYLEY comforts her.

HAYLEY: The neighbour told us... I'm really sorry Cate.

TONY: Y'see I think what I do to survive is fair and you think what you do to survive is fair... not you personally Cate but your family... like your son... being blown to pieces... now I'd want revenge... because as far as I'm concerned it's all a battlefield. I can sing the song like any warrior that I did what I had to do and all that shit... but it's still taking someone's life. Now that's where the difference lies in my opinion. I have integrity because the lives I choose to take are known to me but in the army it's just the enemy... someone you might have a drink with down the pub if circumstances were different... a neighbour even... a decent geezer... I mean Vietnam, Cambodia... tourist destinations... what the fuck!

TONY crosses over to HAYLEY and strokes her pregnant belly.

HAYLEY looks uneasy but tries to cover it.

TONY: (CONT'D) Weekend breaks in Afghanistan for this little bruiser... this little soldier... he's the dude isn't he... he's the future?

TONY turns to CATE. He is quietly aggressive.

TONY: (CONT'D) Whereas John...

Pause

TONY: (CONT'D) ...was spent.

TONY shakes his head in frustration.

CATE is troubled.

CATE: Spent? What do you mean?

TONY: After Lucy left... John was determined to leave the hospital and go to the police... he got quite 'insistent'. Someone had to stop him... like I said when I'm cornered I fight to the ferocious end...

CATE: Are you saying... you did something to John?

TONY: All in the line of duty.

CATE: Did you hurt him?

TONY: I won't lie... I warned him about the leather as well... don't bleed on the pale interior... that concession went out of the window... but then so did John... in a matter of sorts.

CATE tries to make another move to the door.

TONY pushes her back.

CATE: I'm going to have to leave. I've got things to...

TONY: *(interrupting)* You're going nowhere because I am getting tense... and that's not good for me... that 'white heat thing'. You never know where it might lead, how it might end... isn't that right Hayley?

HAYLEY: It's you and me against the world Tone... always has been... always will be... and with the baby on the way... we're invincible.

TONY: That's the word... invincible. You really are a class act babes... isn't she Cate?

CATE shakes her head in acknowledgement.

TONY: (CONT'D) And we're happy aren't we? We're a fucking family... all pulling together in the same direction... aren't we Cate?

CATE does not answer. TONY is insistent.

TONY: (CONT'D) Aren't we Cate?

CATE: *(hesitant)* Yes, we are.

TONY: We are what?

CATE: We're a family.

TONY nods, pleased.

TONY: Not just any family... we're a happy family. *(beat)* No need for anyone... to be sad... anymore.

TONY gets up and goes to his bag and takes out a bottle of Pina Colada, some sunglasses and a hat.

TONY: (CONT'D) I bought a bottle of 'Pina Colada' ...I'm going to make some cocktails. Fancy one Cate? I'll do a virgin one for you Hay'ls... I've got all the trimmings. I've even bought little umbrellas.

TONY puts on the hat and sunglasses.

HAYLEY: It's so hot out there... might as well have them on the patio. I'll put my bikini on.

TONY: *(suggestive)* Now you talking gel... ring my bell.

HAYLEY: *(teasing)* Don't be sexist Tone.

TONY: Sexist you love it.

TONY pats HAYLEY'S bottom and moves into the kitchen.

HAYLEY crosses over to CATE.

HAYLEY: *(confidentially)* Don't pay too much attention to what he says... it's cos he was locked in a cupboard.

HAYLEY exits upstairs.

CATE alone takes a long moment, before speaking quietly to herself.

CATE: I'll do a fish pie later...with some coconut milk. I could make some ice cream as well... I haven't done that in a long time... put some chocolate flakes on top, then we can have 99's... you used to love those when you were a little boy...

TONY enters; he listens as CATE talks.

CATE: (CONT'D) ...especially with strawberry sauce and sprinkles...

TONY: *(interrupting)* I love strawberry sauce and sprinkles... you've found my Achilles heel!

TONY hands CATE a drink with an umbrella.

CATE pauses.

CATE: You should put some sun cream on... if you're going to stay out there... or you'll get burned.

TONY: Dog days, not my favourite time of year to be honest. Everybody goes mental.

CATE looks at TONY closely. She holds his face gently in her hands.

CATE: You're quite fair skinned... the sun probably doesn't agree with you. I've got some total block in the drawer... maybe you'd be better off with that.

TONY: I do have sensitive skin as it happens.

CATE: You're a sensitive boy.

TONY: That's right Ma, I am.

CATE: That's why I'm here... to look after you.

TONY: I need looking after.

CATE: I know you do.

TONY moves off into the kitchen area.

CATE opens the drawer. On top of it is the photograph of PAUL. She looks at it briefly, kisses it and then puts it away.

CATE: (CONT'D) No one... needs to be sad... anymore...

CATE takes out the sun block and exits.
BLACKOUT